Glasses of a POET

Glasses

OF A

POET

R. Angel

Author R. Angel

GLASSES OF A POET

Copyright © 2015 Kim Morrow (R. Angel)

All rights reserved. No part of this book may be reproduced or transmitted in any form or by any means, electronic or mechanical, including photocopying, recording, or by any information storage and retrieval system, without permission in writing from the publisher. All questions and/or request are to be submitted to: 134 Andrew Drive, Reidsville NC, 27320.

To the best of said publisher's knowledge, this is an original manuscript and is the sole property of author **AUTHOR R. ANGEL**

Printed in the United States of America

ISBN-13:978-0692517369
ISBN-10:0692517367

Printed by Createspace 2015
Published by BlaqRayn Publishing Plus 2015

Glasses of a POET

DEDICATION

This book is dedicated to God,
my first love...

All those I love and all those
who know and have
experienced the power of true
love...

R. Angel

Author R. Angel

Introduction

This is my 5th poetry book and this one may be my most heartfelt. It is the result of an encounter that totally and irrevocably changed me as a person, a woman and an artist. There was once a time when I wondered if "unconditional love" was just a phrase or a thought for a past time that no longer exists...
I know now that it is real and it is beautiful to behold.

Glasses of a Poet is a collection of poetry from the soul of Author R. Angel, that chronicles her transformation due to the revelation of seeing herself in the reflection of someone else's eyes..

Glasses of a POET

Glasses

OF A

POET

R. Angel

Glasses of a POET

SEEN

You saw me before I saw you...laced in possibility and possible intimacy, you tracked me...discovered and uncovered me, now in my vulnerability I see you...the true that others cannot or are not allowed to view...embraced by your pain and the enduring duress of stress, you traced the lines that contain your hurt with art...your bruised and broken heart spilling lines of ink like blood...in a tidal wave, tsunami or flood, it pours from your veins...oozes from your brain as your mind releases the pieces of a shattered soul, yet through all that fog, you saw me, stuck in the mud and bog of my depression, my emotions in deep recession and abused...you saw me and...

Author R. Angel

Refused to let me sink in the stink of self-pity and doubt without a fight...giving up hope and finding a way out, you saw me and the rescuer in you began to speak...softly, with the gentleness of the meek and the passion of a pursuer you spoke, putting my thoughts on pause and the license of imminent doom on revoke.. lifting the dark of a lonely room with a smile to cloak your own gloom and repression...you lit the coals that would later ignite a blaze...invite a crazed hunger for the written and spoken word, a love for poetry to one day unfold...

Then you began to mold the artist in me...the creator of things blind and hidden...things I couldn't see...things I once thought

Glasses of a POET

forbidden or for others...my mind became the ground for your seed, my soul the holder of your unrevealed need to bleed and give...my thoughts, your abode...the place where you live and breed more dreams like visions, your words became my meals upon which I would feed and you kept my mental pantry full of provisions...

But now, in my strength, I see you...in the strong that you procured and secured, I visualize the words I internalized so long ago...Now I see, I hear, I know and I capitalize on the knowing, owing it all to you and you showing me the way. I see you and what was once put on pause for me can now repeat its feat for you...to bring you the new life which is your due.

Author R. Angel

Night and day, you dug into the earth of my hard and dry life to plant your seed…it went deep… God says it is time for you to reap the life…the hope that you have sown…I see u, fully, completely because you saw me…

Therefore, I will do what He has sent me to do…I see u and before too long, the entire world will see you too…

Glasses of a POET

Twisted

Twisting, turning, weaving...forever reasoning
Thought manipulating movement like seasoning...
Flavoring and teasing the mental palette...delicately
Enhancing the taste of verbal interaction...a reaction to
The hint of spice in the language and glow of conversation
That higher stimulation outside of body and into soul...to mold
And hold the attention of even the shortest span...

Ink covered hands create bands that wrap the mind in vise like time warps and metaphors the process of thinking...inking ideas and plans, written strategies, demands requisite and

Author R. Angel

intricate rhymes...fine lines that spell out dreams, hopes and wishes, serving up dishes of aromatic food for thought...laying out doubt on paper thin and crisp...tracing faith and love in wisp of nostalgic loops and twirls...quill swirls to produce the creative juice flow to get just the appropriate mixture... Blood and ink...the elixir of the writer...Pain and survival...the weapons of the fighter...love and brokenness...the wings of the night rider...the constant insider who sees and hears all then scribes it on the walls of the heart...the joys and sorrows...the fullness and hollows of life's continuous beat...

This is the writer's passion...his heat...to lay

Glasses of a POET

pearls of words like dew drops and gems at our feet...to cater to our whims and fantasies as they hide their own within their written eccentricities...allowing intimacies only possible through spoken and inked intercourse, feeling no shame, apologies or remorse for they are the story tellers...they are bold..

And as old as the world in its orbit around the universe...so they twist us, turn us, weave us...forever reasoning and seasoning us with their diverse flavors...presenting us with hand-crafted favors we savor after each dialect-able meal...for they are the Scribes of how we feel in a place all too real, they twist us with a thrill and give us black gold chills that help us climb the

Author R. Angel

hills of daily living...forever
inking, forever
twisting...forever giving...

Glasses of a POET

The Rim of Glasses

I often wonder how I will look reflected in your glasses as the ice breaks and clinks against the rim...brimming over with the pure smoothness of Hennessy and your words light to the touch and easy going down yet packing a power punch leading to a late brunch and even later supper... folk are used to breakfast in bed but let's take the head, I'll let you lead and do a late night meal in bed instead...

Enjoying fruit so juicy and tender, the type that makes you surrender to the nectar spilling down your chin and the pleasure it produces within...a late munch that continues until the morning light, thinking about the conversation that turned into

Author R. Angel

a night of let's take flight and let our anatomies talk...they have been silent for so long, but they have a song they yearn to sing, a note they wish to explore, natural wine they ache to drink, dipping in designs of ink intricately woven on fevered skin...to spill our thrills on lined and linen sheets, writing a poetry as old as time as we cross that thin line and you bring me to the brink of losing my mind and being hungry for more...devouring each delicate morsel of eat em up, filling the lips of my awaiting cup with the water of your potency, your eyes mirror me and the rise in my thighs they cry to see...

Vision so clear and crystal as to look through the outer to penetrate the inner and

Glasses of a POET

calculate the tight entrance...the maze unbreached, you maneuver your way inside my pride where I hide all my secret treasures and fantasy pleasures are revealed to your skilled tongue and masterful hands like a captain at the helm of a drenched ship, with one placed on hip, you guide her through the deep throes of passion's keep...whipping the stern as she flips and turns to your experienced ministration...

You are focused, but she has lost all concentration as tongue gently licks tips...moans escape lips that have been locked for what seems an eternity...whispered demands in listening ears...years of build up and love like lust procuring thrust

Author R. Angel

into I must have you in me...deeply and ever growing...knowing the eruption and corruption of these walls will reap the waterfall you seek... your need speaks and my need fulfills...giving and receiving...releasing and retrieving ...catching and throwing until the explosion rips...the time/space continuum slips...our collective orgasm trips from mouths open, hearts clanging and planets banging against one another as one completes and depletes the other...seconds stand still to push away the moment when this bliss must end...but wait, we have a lifetime to press repeat and begin again...

Glasses of a POET

Blank Page...

Trying to decide what to write
tonight
as the moon dances with the
stars and I
wonder where you are and
what you may be
doing...are u pursuing your
dreams and the grand
schemes you plan for yourself
or are you pursuing
another...to make her your
lover as I sit in limbo...
waiting to know the outcome
of what was done and the
foolishness of my
mistake...earnestly wishing to
take back
the last few days...make them
vanish away and disappear
with
the hurt I hear in your every
word...I was ohhh so wrong
and the
words of the song were so

Author R. Angel

precious to me...I just didn't see the
trouble I was making and the route you were taking was not the
usual path...I should have done the math but we have not equaled
anything but business for so very long that I misconstrued feelings
so strong and trust issues so deep...I should have been alert but I was
asleep in thinking I knew what you wanted between me and you and what
you wanted me to do that I missed the change.. now it has all been
rearranged...so I'm left soaking in my guilt and the wilt and tilt of what
I once had...left feeling abandoned and bad...the truth ringing loud and

Glasses of a POET

sad in my ears as I wipe away
tears that have drenched the
skin I'm in
because I have disappointed
you yet again...

I have damaged and bruised
something so dear to
me...misused and abused an
intimacy few ever know will
be...hurt and mishandled the
one
thing near to my heart...too
late it became clear to me and
see...I don't know how to
rectify the situation...reverse
the direction of your thoughts
towards us...bring you back to
a place where you are at least
willing to
discuss and not fuss and to
forgive me for my deed...I
would plead my case for
loving you but there is no
need...you already know I do...

Author R. Angel

So I sit in limbo waiting to know the outcome of what I've done from the only one that can save me and save the remnants of reality born from my deepest fantasy as the ink of our pain stains this blank page...

Glasses of a POET

Sounds of Love

Symphonies of sound
bombard my
hearing...melodies of moans,
animalistic groans of pleasure
as your powerful thrusts
invade my lust...my eyes
tearing from the sheer bliss of
your southern kiss...
take me...
take me now...
take me with you...
arch my back...bend me to
your will...the ink of my wet
longs for the dip of your quill...
fuck me,
lick me,
corrupt these sheets with me...
entice me...
seduce me...
once, twice...reduce me to a
mass of quivering, quaking
nerve endings tingling with
Sinsation and shaking with
the mingling of our deep

Author R. Angel

penetration...mentally
stroking the clit of my mind
while your tongue tips the lips
of my womanly grind and you
drink me...

Inhale the sweet heat of me
while I drench your face with
the intoxicating lace of my
silky cream...never in our
wildest dream could we have
imagined this...
this twist...
this boiling mix of insatiable
schemes and positions
galore...you got me begging
for more of that dic-licious
treat between my feet and my
raised hips you grip with such
force as you graze inside my
pasture like a lost but found
sheep...inch by inch you
creep...finding that g-spot of
hot lava gushing...waters
rushing to meet the pulsing
throb of your meat...

Glasses of a POET

inhibitions no more...restraint
like clothes thrown carelessly
to the floor...we been at it
since you stepped through the
door with not one complaint...
stripped me...
flipped me...
doggy-style whipping
until you had me dripping
Ate your dinner...then licked
your plate
Damn, my Kat can't wait til
the next pen meets paper
date...

Author R. Angel

Stuck

It was the sex that did it...yep...hmm-hmm...dicked me just right, hit it then told me to quit it...had me cumming to his tune...ass high to the moon and on fire and all he would require is that I talk dirty when he was licking that purty putty tat and smacking that g-spot like that...like that...

It was the "D" that fukked me...had me stuck like Chuck see...I couldn't figure what was the trigger until my body gave me the signal every time he stepped in the room...like boom...cosmic explosions and implosions...pussy gushing...nerves tingling like pins to a pin cushion...blood pressure rushing to all the erogenous zones...hormones and pheromones acting a

Glasses of a POET

fool...couldn't wait to wrap my lips around his power tool...both sets all wet and dripping like a lioness in wait for her prey to come tipping and slip in my trap...enjoying his delicacies all night and day...

It was the tongue that hooked me...when he flicked it kinda crooked and took it to the clit...I be loving that shit and kitty be spitting them serious spits and juicing things up while Babyboy flips that cup to his lips and drinks me in...all my passion and Sin spilling and filling his goblet with my droplets of pure sensual elixir...our own special mixture and blend...others can't comprehend the addiction...the fixation...his loving is better than any yoga or meditation cause I'm so

Author R. Angel

into his deep penetration and oral ministration... the highland scream when we release our inner ice cream that melts and flows until it's lusciously sticky...

I told y'all it was the sex...drugs me like a mickie...

Glasses of a POET

The Ordinary Hero

I feel you as if you were real sometimes...not just a figment of my very real imagination...gestating and fermenting in my mind...a figure of endless time and space...you consume whole blocks of my creative process as your fingertips caress the limbs of my thoughts to relieve the stress of wanting what does not truly exist...the phantom whisper of a kiss and passion strokes that choke out all reason and conscious assumption...until reality forces the resumption of everyday life and the urgent needs of daily deeds required for survival yet night fall hails your arrival and the twist in damp sheets as the nocturnal dance repeats itself again and again...it's hard to comprehend

Author R. Angel

and understand how one could so long for and love the burning hands of an invisible Superman...

Wet my dreams with the waters of your essence and I will wet your reality with the juices of my flesh...Let's mesh and fuse in the luscious ooze of sexual delights...the thrill of victory in each other's heights and the pounding lust in each thrust of our wanton pens...cum again? Say cum again...it would be my pleasure as I fulfill yours to the max...relax...I got this...I got the answer to your question's bliss...I got the solution to your body's problem of fatigue and restlessness...right here under my dress as we hinge on the outskirts of momentous climax...just as you eased out

Glasses of a POET

of those slacks and pushed
aside the thong with deep,
long strokes of your hardened
quill...pushing your agenda as
you bend me over to your
will...cum again? Say cum
again as you swallow my
intimate pill and send a
massive chill up my arched
spine...I will cum again and
again til you release all that is
mine and you drink every
drop like the finest of sweet
wine...

Shadows cast light upon the
walls of my glistening
room...the hero enters like in a
dream...the state between two
worlds ripped a part at the
seam of my conscious ability
to tell real from fantasy...but
see, the hero has come to
rescue me from the mundane
and vain of sexual
mediocrity...from those one

Author R. Angel

minute men and little boy dates and so called "grown and sexy" who can't dine off the plate...the hero has come to deliver and redeem...to turn sighs into yells and moans into "I scream"..."baby please don't stop"...as he delves into the mound of goodies for that last drip drop of cum for me...I need to see you squirm and lose control as my tongue takes hold of your clit and makes you have a fit of frenzy like never before...the phantom of your imaginings just walked through the door...to whisk your inhibitions and fears away...inside your body I long to breath and stay...

So Superman came with invisible hands now solid and whole...taking my body on a stroll down mind boggling

Glasses of a POET

lane...releasing years of pent up frustration and pain and splashing my spirit in the cool of his breeze and the glow of his flow with practiced ease of perfect administrations and just right "u hit the spot" penetrations...oral stimulus an added plus...leaving me completed and depleted and in utter delight as my Superman in poet's clothing flew off into the night...

Author R. Angel

Needs

His needs, her needs...their needs could be met if he would stop playing at being shy and absorbed and get to the root...the core of the situation...it demands deep penetration and serious demonstration...enough with the meditation and contemplation...

They both want, need the feel...to know it's real and not some figment of pure imagination...not some product of verbal stimulation that left her wet and him all hard and set...the implications of passion unbridled and untamed...no need to entertain shame or embark on the blame game...it is what it is...must we give it a name...

Glasses of a POET

Lust in every thrust...in every inward motion of the hips and the licking of the lips as words like foreplay drip from tongues inflamed...thoughts maimed by deeds and hints of promised bliss...the tingle of a first kiss...as flesh meshes to mingle and dance in fevered twists...urges to resist will cease and desist as soon as eyes glimpse the prize and cheeks rise to receive the gift... Legs lift...thighs part...the ancient ritual starts...man and woman become one under the night sun and the stars...as it was meant from the first...the universe smiles and burst into brilliant light as the two take flight on wings of sexual delight to soar higher than the moon...

Pounding...plunging...diving into the center of each

other...giving and taking to and from one another a satisfaction and gratification that goes much deeper than mere sensation...every touch, a dream...every move, a tag team in tandem, nothing random or by mistake as the earth quakes in the wake of this molten shake...this creamy mixture of allure and sure bodily union...

His needs...her needs...their needs could easily be met in the tight of his grip and the slip of her wet...the desire is peaking...heat missiles are loose and seeking the hot of her walls...his body screams, it calls and she has the answer...the ultimate solution but he's still struggling with confusion and disillusion...all I can say is stay tuned for the conclusion...

The Resurrection of Dreams

A dream doesn't stop with the beating of a heart...it simply starts the process of a new dreamer...emerging from the purging that occurs when death introduces it's ice cold fingers of blue fire and reduces one earthly vessel to dust...it's a must that another rise from the ashes...like the phoenix in sync with time and the rhythms of space...another visionary must take its' place in the legendary modules of eternity...

Hell is a dread we all must endure...read your Bible if you are unsure...Sheol (hell) is simply the grave...the tomb...to which we all journey the moment we exit the

Author R. Angel

womb...the moment we breath life...death steps into the race...awaiting the moment we meet face to face; however, death does not determine the parameters of living...the good things of life are for the taking and the giving...you and only you can decide your true fate...whether you agree or negate the fact is your destiny is your own to wield...your dimensions of faith your only shield against untamed tongues desperate for fresh blood to spill...

So take up your sword and the power in your words...your weapons on this battlefield, understanding the birth of your dreams your enemy seeks to kill...as long as you remain silent, ignorant and blind...you also remain safe

Glasses of a POET

from lying lips and plotting minds...but once you allow the scales to fall from your eyes and realize you are the dying of your future...only through YOU can it be revived and survive the death of a dream...

Author R. Angel

THE STUDIO

He stands before the Mic...tall and strong...covered in ink...a trickle of sweat dripping...his words dipping into the pool of her soul...so bold and raw...he saw through her mask to complete the task of opening her mind...

He stands before the Mic...smooth grooving and moving to the beat of the musiq and his muse...refusing to be denied the power in his lyrical language...so fine as he keeps time with the rhyme and sway of her hips...

He stands before the Mic...enticing her with his lips and words so hot as to ignite her mental g-spot...hitting it just right as creative wisdoms flow...he gives her a "Yes I

Glasses of a POET

know" stare and strips her
bare with eyes on fire...

He stands before the
Mic...heightening her desire
and the moisture between her
thighs...where lies the
ultimate prize...will it be
tonight...will passion finally
take flight...soaring through
the air...to feel the graze of his
hand...

He stands before the Mic...this
man of her fantasy...to let him
enter her and see the depths of
her deep and levels of
intimacy beyond his wildest
dreams...it's hot as hell in the
room as sexual tensions clash
and boom...

He stands before the Mic...it
seems she's squirming now
and twitching as his manhood
looms erect...her insides

Author R. Angel

itching to be scratched by that small thatch of hair on his chin...tongue licking to delve into the sweetness of her patch...

Sex flares from within...no longer able to ignore or fight this plight...the erotic dance begins...she willingly becomes the cup into which he will pour his water and she will gladly drink...juices flowing like ink as together they recite...now...as

THEY lay before the Mic!

Glasses of a POET

No Truer Love

A Truer, Rarer Love
Old love gone..
New love awaiting
To find me home and
anticipating the new road
We'll roam together...loving
One another while forsaking
All others and taking our time
To explore our rhythm and
rhyme...
Blowing each other's minds to
the tune
Of our own beat...massaging
feet and
Soaking sheets in our own
twisting dance
Of endless romance and
explosive passion
At a glance...we chance to take
it higher...to
Fly on wings of our desire and
see what's next...
To write the unwritten text of
our story in all it's flame

Author R. Angel

And glory...disappointments
and hurt...joys and pain...
Rays of sunshine and
downpours of drenching rain...
Clinching and un-clinching
our unflinching hearts in
Each line of every part as the
saga unfolds...mysteries
Untold revealed before our
very eyes, undisguised as
Dreams erupt between moist
thighs and realities are
Born in tight places within
hardened spaces of piercing
Fire...to feel each touch and
the power of each thrust
Produced by the juices of lust
and much needed
Attention...grasping lengthy
dimensions to dive into
Oceans of love's potions,
getting lost in grinds of epic
motion hour by hour...
Old love is gone...
Faded, vanished and
Spent, yet in its place a

Glasses of a POET

Truer, rarer love has been
Sent... so no pining and wishing
Precious time away...look up and
Enjoy the dawn of a new day. Wait..
Be patient...your opportunity will knock
Again...For love stands at the door...
Open up and let him in...

Author R. Angel

Hidden Beauty

I went to the store of my feelings and purchased a huge supply of love, joy, patience and kindness to help me deal with times of stress and to ward off the cloak of depression that often threatens to fall when life calls on us to live in the world of reality...I'd rather escape to the world of fantasy with you and do loops around Saturn's rings, dip toes in cooling springs of dreams and desires...those sorts of things but it seems the pull of real is like strings binding us...pulling us back to the natural when the Super is what we crave...unwilling slaves to the responsibility of achieving, yet foolishly believing we can escape the

Glasses of a POET

ordeal and feel the hands of Freedom caress our Soul's flesh and undress our bondage wraps, removing the steel traps of mundane existence in the presence of the divine so we can combine with the elements of purest pleasure and become one...it has begun...the weaving of fantasies web as we flow and ebb on a current moved by invisible force through an invincible Source that refuses to let us drown and be held down...the oppressed...under duress yet determined to pass the test others have failed...not willing to let plans, hopes, goals derail on this track called life...shouldering the strife and burden like a boulder as days get shorter and nights grow colder... the sun continues to shine...the moon continues to beam...we continue to dream

Author R. Angel

the fantasy dream and as long as we close our eyes and see great things, we can possess all the beauty life holds and brings...

Glasses of a POET

You Too Can Love Again

Daring my heart to trust again...my soul to open its windows to the light within your smile...all the while wondering when the shoe would drop and the top blow clean off the roof...waiting for the truth to hit the tattered remnants of my peace...holding that inhaled breath that so needed release from the shattered shards, a broken piece of what I once was...to exhale the thin air of haunted time and memories that defined the lining of my dreams...deferred and deterred by lack of support...they were sport to the mindless, careless beings they once entertained, yet in the midst of the storm,

Author R. Angel

hail and rain of pain...some small hope remained...

Drama caused stress and trauma to the best of my plans... misunderstands and unheard of demands were more than the heart could stand so I sat in my fault...in the reprimands, fermenting like malt liquor in its aged brine and keg...we were on our last leg, tittering to fall...u failing to heed the call of a love battered and bruised...refusing to diffuse the bomb that was US, and the impending explode...my overcharged system declaring "Overload!"

It blew...and with it went me and you...gone with the wind...scattered among the ashes of recurring

Glasses of a POET

Sin...committed in the den of your selfishness and my foolishness...but I have come to realize it was for the best...best that we end the mess we had become...the hum drum of lies and deceits...the maelstrom of hollow victories and filled defeats...it was time...time to change the rhythm...the rhyme in our not so equal dance...we gambled and lost the roll...the dice requiring we fold...our story had been told...

Inside the crumbled recesses of my soul...passion still burned...low and without any real warmth...my fire was cold but the embers were patient, lying in wait for the descent of the wood that would add to the life of the sad flickering flame and ignite in me that

Author R. Angel

blaze with a name...Love...to love again...to embrace the fine lace of desire and take a chance to soar higher...above the ashes like that majestic bird rises from the devastation and dust...to grasp the thrust of manic lust mixed with purest, raw feeling...that is what he offered.. the poetry of Love again...

Silky words on ink filled pages...images of mages old and new...to be bold where once being careful was the thing to do...to say "screw you depression" and end the regression of a forward thinking being and plunge head first...without blinking...into waters that would quench my thirst by only making me hungrier...to look into the potent, molten

Glasses of a POET

eyes of my adore and know
that this was real...no one
night thrill...but the very chill
that climbs my spine each
time his thoughts inner twine
with mine. My cells were on
burst the first time we inked,
from his cup of lyrical nectar I
drinked and am still
drinking...wine flutes clinking
as we celebrate the rapture
within...daring my heart to
trust and love again...

Author R. Angel

Ink Stained Lovers

Memories like puppets pull strings, rings around Saturn as you orbit my space...my heartbeat races to catch a glimpse of your man in the moon...let's walk through the stars as we wait for the clouds to usher in the blue skies and the rays of sunshine... I don't mind just basking in your glow...the flow of your essence laces me like silk and diamond drops...each tear a treasure as I long to have you near me...Hear me...the pleasure in the sound of your voice...

I am moist to the touch of your hand...we escape to the lands and isles of what could be...the scape of dream and fantasy when reality is too real and the air too still to feel

Glasses of a POET

the cool breeze of possibility...we transcend and transform...too out of the ordinary and norm to conform to this melodramatic world...we cannot be broken so we bend but to our own beat...to our own tempo and dance we twirl...when the lives we are living takes more than giving and we seek solace...we run to the canvas of the mind to release...to unchain our bonds and find peace in the stroke...in the pen and the ink...we make love on fine lined sheets...beds, floors and counter-tops of words become intimate points of rendezvous for lovers to mate and participate in the bleeding...

"I adore and mi amore" translate into "I love you boo"...it is all the same for passion's sake...

Author R. Angel

The moment comes when the light of imagination is receding and the realm of bills and responsibility slams the door of make believe and the lovers must separate...they must leave
the canvas incomplete ...retreat behind the masks that help them perform their daily tasks with a bit of efficiency until they can meet again...to spend countless hours locked in the power of their written romance...building words like braille to help them see the beauty in a world full of empty...full of malice, hate and strife...the canvas of their creation to ease the ache of devastation and disappointment, their ink-letting like ointment to soothe the cuts and bruises of all the mistreatment and abuses at the hands of this life.

Glasses of a POET

They masturbate lines and cum so beautifully together when their juices mesh like the lyrics of their favorite song...one day flesh will become the paper upon which they write..their souls will truly take flight into a night that never ends...a continuous rhyme that makes its own time and the painting brushed by their ink spill will become all too real...

Author R. Angel

Love Is..

Love...if it has to be spoken it is a mere empty token of the true

Love...should be shown in and out of view

Love..should take you to places you've never been

Love...erotic, exotic places without and within

Love...should be counted as priceless year round

Love...visual and tangible, not just syllables you sound

Glasses of a POET

Love...should wash away the stench of a horrid day

Love...should make invisible notes to a song play continuously in your soul

Love...that knows no bounds but grows and grows and grows, never growing old

Love...never becoming tired and weary of the weight of showing itself, taken off the shelf of the mundane and just getting over

Love...is like a fresh new dawn to discover and uncover those things hidden deep within each other

Love may just have to say "I'm sorry...I apologize" because only with the

Author R. Angel

understanding of love do we realize our potential to hurt another, aiding the demise and diminishing of our character in their eyes.

Love's place is not only between open thighs and drenched sheets..love is the rhythm that beats in the heart to cause passions to rise...higher than the mountain or the passion's peak for it is true love true lovers seek...love brings boldness to the humble and meek...it brings humbleness to the arrogant and chic...love is a language only the Spirit can speak and only the Spirit can recognize where the heart of true love lies.

It rest not in the words of the untrue, the abused and

Glasses of a POET

misused "I love you"... it best not be found in the roving, exploring hand of that woman or man only looking to fulfill their fleshly lust.

It Must be visible in the forward and ever moving thrust of action and deed...it feeds the need of giver as well as receiver...making a true believer of them both...they succumb to the mutual, silent calls of a love that shatters illusions and tears down walls...a love that cannot and will not be ignored, but demands being acknowledged, embraced, adored and poured out like life saving water upon ground thirsty to drink...a love that soaks like ink upon paper, that strokes like paint upon canvas...a love that inspires, creates and thinks.

Author R. Angel

For without upward thought and progression, no love can survive...it is from the evolving will in each that true love must derive in order to remain alive.

Glasses of a POET

Hues of Seduction

Midnight's wanton canvas
paints my pleasures
in vivid colors of orgasmic
eruptions...hues of my
seductions...

Bright yellows and red...the
visual treasures of my desire...
palette of fires deep in the gut
as we lie upon this bed and
contemplate...come participate
in my hues of seduction...

Hush...shut up...be quiet and
be still...give in to my will as
the
patterns take shape...the
brilliant light to drape limbs
entwined as
I climb to find his rock...don't
you dare mock my hues of
seduction...

Author R. Angel

Tick Tock strikes the clock as we are lost in the picture we create...
time forgotten and stolen...love organs swollen and throbbing as we mate...mixing the perfect tint to the hues of my seduction...

I rest upon his easel and await the brush of his pen stroke to seal my
fate... pastel and blush...don't make too much fuss...the masterpiece
soon to reveal...Oh yes he can feel my hues of seduction...

A shapely leg here...a thick thigh there...toes pointed in the air...I encircle
his tool with the greatest of care...a nipple hardened by a touch...tongues
dance a jig...we wanted so much...these are a few hues of my seduction...

Glasses of a POET

A moan of pleasure...a gush of sweet juice...it really takes all this to produce...
the abstract drawing...a collector's dream...the scream as the lust builds and mounts...I want it all...no buyer discounts...lost in my hues of seduction...

The canvas is wet...the painting complete...a master at his craft...he drenched every sheet...he brought my yelps of climax to quivering reduction...how?...
my master poet has his own hues of Seduction...

Author R. Angel

Just Me

Dine, wine and grind is fine for some women but I like it hard core...the scream for more that comes from down and dirty how we do it in the South...your mouth tasting the smooth of my pudding groove and licking the edges of the pop...can't call me a tart cause I'm sweet like a Georgia peach when you reach to squeeze the tight and don't find no lumps...that mixture has been stirred to perfection...my confectioners sugar got you drooling...spit pooling at the base and I can hear your drum beat...ba boom...the full treatment just stepped in the room to give you some special attention to them honorable mentions, those family

Glasses of a POET

jewels...them shed house tools that need a good greasing and some accurate pleasing from my Dirty South mouth, but I'll stay off my knees cause your name ain't Jeeee...sus.

You tease and fuss over trivial shit...I just want you to hit it from the back with a smack...yeah...I like it like dat. These other chicks playing that game cause they crave your last name but baby, I'm just craving that good in your goody and that wood in your woody wood pecker, that nasty home wrecker to blowout my back like that powerful Black & Decker blower, chop down my weeds with your riding mower and riding is what we gone do when I get my hands on you. I got insight into your needs like I been reading a book and

Author R. Angel

imma cook up a meal to satisfy all your desires, squirt my water to put out all your fires and make you wonder why you never gave this a try before. That squeaking door ain't the sound of you leaving but you coming back for more...

Pour my juices on you like rain in the summer...fuck around and heal that heart murmur as your soul expands under the caress of my hands and my sensual demands as each touch eases a nerve that's been twitching, fist clenched and un-clenching from the tension and stress of life...the daily strife of just living...well I got a receiver for your giving, a glove for them balls and a shake that will relax your every ache and muscle...so after a hard day of the grind

Glasses of a POET

and hustle...slide between my
feet and my cool cotton sheets
for that rejuvenating tussle
and be reminded of what it's
like to feel like a Man

Author R. Angel

Every Breath She Breathes

(A Collaboration)

Kim Morrow

She wants him. With every breath she breathes, she wants him but it must be mutual and it isn't. So, she will come and basks in his presence for an hour, maybe two then she will depart, cherishing that hour or two for the rest of time with every breath she breathes...

Why Yet

Because his eyes command her immediate attention. His confidence bargains with no one. The baritone sandalwood that lives in his voice bows to nothing yet is loving and

Glasses of a POET

respectful. His magnetism is greased lightning and she has been struck...

Kim

And stuck like glue to the pure real in his swag...the genuine in his speech as he lays words at her feet like pearls and diamonds to drape and embrace her thoughts. He has opened the door of her mind and entered a realm he breached with finesse and wisdom, making her see impossibilities possible simply because he speaks it..she reflects on the calm in his quiet storm, the gentle whirlwind that loosed her bonds and released her creativity to flow like the sweetest water from the fountain of his care...

Author R. Angel

Why Yet

His mental stimulation is an exotic computation of life's realities made plain to see. Mixing his words like a creamed sundae and spoon feeding the magnitude of her blessing in small bites. Teasing her hunger while quenching her mental thirst for knowledge. She is temporarily satisfied...

Kim

And there they remain...giving and receiving, releasing and retrieving in this dance of words and romance...each step...each bite rendering them closer to the completion of the final act in this play...this story told but unlike Romeo and Juliet..their love is bold and as old as time itself. The end will surely

Glasses of a POET

come as all endings must...the final curtain call, the final thrust into infamy but until that moment, this remains their reality, a living, thriving dream with a plot, a scheme so full of twists as to turn the head of the greatest storytelling buff...this is the stuff of Hollywood, it would seem, but they live it daily and daily they shall continue til the culmination explodes and each is totally gratified...

Janae PoeticSoul Stewart

Gratified to sing of a heart unspoken
Love of them a sort that is told with their first token
As just the sentiments of a kiss on a hand made their hearts beat as one
Seeing even in the darkness
The bright light of the sun

Author R. Angel

And adventure with just a
little step
He and she hold hands only
with the
smelling of each other's
radiant breath...

Rosalind Cherry

He was stuck and struck, he
was there
longing for her embrace, she
was missing him too, their
kisses upon their lips, he was
staring as if she missed his
touches upon her skin then the
door opens, soft winds upon
her flesh.. what a rush.. then
he whispered for her to hush..
all the open wounds begin to
heal.. He touched her face, she
touched his as the candles
blew in the midst of the night..
he took her by the waist she
fell into his arms, soft kisses
upon her neck, she wrapped

Glasses of a POET

her leg around his thigh, it
was to be their natural high.
They could not help what
they were feeling that look
they had staring into each
other's eyes.. he took her there,
unfolding into their personal
paradise.. she ending the
message in soft moans as she
bites and sucks upon his ears..
he held on for dear life.. she
says let go.. he says I can't.. no
more lies my beloved, for I
love you, I shall never let you
go as she was struck by words
she longed to hear from him..
she whispers "take me to a
place where we lock into this
forbidden love and unchain
links that make us whole.."

Author R. Angel

Raw Expression

"Talk is cheap but I will break this hundred dollar bill and leave you the cents for the expense of you running that mouth...shut the hell up and catch the train down south...my Georgia peach is ripe and juicy...so let your fingers do the talking..as your tongue does the walking in and out my fruity mound...you better get to spitting if you looking to ground and pound..."

Glasses of a POET

One Night

The creamy, smooth blend...tiny pearl drops of heaven...seven plus two is the measure in inches...kitty flinches just a bit every time he enters her glistening gates...he waits until she is primed and wet from the erotic pump of her hormones and the pheromones working to achieve just the perfect puddle...

afterwards they would cuddle and coo but right now it's time to do what they came here for...saliva slick kisses pour like rain upon her neck and breast...feet to chest and knees bending, rendering and surrendering her goodies to all he brings to the table...more than able to feed the need

Author R. Angel

pounding through her veins
and the yearning burning like
inferno flames inside her heat
laced lady...penetrating the
core of her being and her soul
with each bold, renewed
thrust of his hips...

she is captivated...mesmerized
by the fire in his eyes and his
wandering tongue upon her
tips...her walls gripping the
throbbing ache of his passion
as every plunge takes him
deeper into the place of their
salvation...their healing...each
dive repairing the breach in
hearts...each moan meant to
reach into the essence of
them...restoring what was
once ripped apart and torn...a
rhythm is born...a pace set by
desire and lust...by pain and
loneliness...by neglect and
abject rejection...

Glasses of a POET

the power of his erection
filling her to the brim...the
rim of her cup lost in the
massive flood his love
produces...she is willing to
give him all...thrilling in the
demands of his body and
hands as he reclaims no man's
land and makes her totally his
own... completely violating
her inner spaces...robbing her
of coherent and descent
thought as her lips scream
obscenities, he uses his fingers
to tease her aching clit til she
whispers "Please..."

He knows what she wants yet
the torture is so sweet...the
exquisite ecstasy etched on her
face...a pleasure to meet. His
goal is to make her cum and
cum again before he gives in
to the rising urge in every
surge, in every dip in her tight

Author R. Angel

juices...she will climb walls
before the curtain falls but
there's no running...no way of
escape... he will manipulate
and play her body like
a sheet awaiting his fine
ink...drum out his beats on her
plump cheeks...deplete and
send her into peaceful
slumber...under her pillow...in
the morn, she will find his
private number...

Glasses of a POET

Mouth Full of Expression

Drink in the essence of my flavor as you enjoy and savor every drip when you dip the tip of your tongue into the wet of my pool...shit so sweet it makes you drool at the mere thought of my gear and the junk in my high end trunk...running traces like paces over and around my clit...that spot you just hit...hit it again as we get into the thick of it...my patience running thin and my temp on high...not a dry place on these sheets as inch by inch you drench my lady with your spit...

Author R. Angel

Chocolate Expression

Thick chocolate thighs...got that mist in your eyes while your dick is on the rise waiting to hear my cries of abandon and surrender but can you render my ass powerless and out of control...do you hold the key to unlock the door of my inner freak...that bitch ain't meek or mild, she will keep you grinding for a good long while but first...u gotta burst that bubble in her fucking mind...you gotta bring it and stimulate the clit of her thinking...hit the g-spot of her thought process unless you don't stand a chance to shadow dance with this piece...no romance or release if you can't penetrate her intellect and open the legs of her intelligence...hence making her juices flow to yo

Glasses of a POET

unique dialect and discourse
that leads to an intercourse
outside the realm of human
existence. See she is a divine
queen...can you glean her
royalty from her hint of the
intimacies that lie between
her chocolate, sweating thigh
that fits perfectly against your
ear..oh dear...did you hear
what she said...your head
game had better be tight while
you lick the nether lips of her
brain stem just right and she
rides the way of your cum to
me all night...

Author R. Angel

Highlights of a Climax

Climbing climatic mountains to reach peaks so sleek and highs...butter pecan thighs wrapped tight around sighs and moans...growls and groans of pleasure escape as his seeking tongue finds hidden treasure buried deep within...teeth lightly scrape lips moist with womanly nectar...he receives...it drips...his oral cup dips to taste the tangy sweetness...drinking in the completeness of her glory... over and over to repeat this invading madness...his only goal...to bring her to trembling climax...
Relax...be still...let me ease your body into this with practiced expertise... remember you are the tease

Glasses of a POET

that wanted to appease the beast in me, so allow the beast to set your body and inner freak free...let my oral ministrations loosen your inhibitions until the urge to resist no longer exist and you open wide for me... let my finger funking tangle in your hairs and jangle you nerves as I caress them curves and lick them breast til your mind bends and swerves around my cause and effect...you ain't came yet...I want it sloppy and soaking wet...that kat must gush at the thought of my touch...at the rush of my stroke...making a mad dash cause you know imma smash dat ass...you get all hot and flush...shiiiiitttt, the plans I got for you would make a porn star blush...so relax...we just getting started...open both mouths...I want all lips parted

Author R. Angel

as I bring you to screaming climax...

I've gone to heaven or I must be dreaming cause his tongue is among the stars as he glides it around and inside my milky way...I'm creaming and the universe is ripping...dude got me tripping...flipping on some cosmic shit...my pussy ain't spit like this since forever and a day...but I gotta play it cool and skool him on my A+ head game...make him scream my fucking name and be all fucked up and sprung...but...I gotta wait til this nicca get done...his private conversation with my intimate parts is causing agitations on a much deeper note...got high pitches coming from my throat...I wanna feel that throbbing rod hit the sensitive spot on my clit...I'm telling you this shit

Glasses of a POET

feels just right...glad I kept it tight...walls gotta be gripping...no slipping as we cum in utter, depleting climax...

The clash and clutter of opposition is gone...all fours is the right position for this doggy style pipe about to be laid...time for the Piper to be paid for all the trash you talked...it's being chalked up to who will tap out first...I hope you rehearsed your lines for telling me I'm the best you had...cause I'm bout to beat this pussy up real bad, so be glad I respect and cherish the woman in you, however, the freak in me is gonna do what he do...your lips are glistening, pulsing, open and I'm listening to the call of your walls...beckoning me to enter, penetrate and give you the

Author R. Angel

reckoning you so richly deserve...I will concentrate all my manly effort on making you squirt as many times as I wish...what a tasty ass dish you already served...now for the main course...you are a sweet morsel...a feast fit for a king so cum here, let's do this damn thing...

The Cadillac rolls into the awaiting hole...lubricated with inner juices and his spit, it produces a sucking noise as she takes him all in...shit, it's a tight fit as the friction of the dance begins...the shaft invades her entrance...hitting spots she forgot were there...her only indication...that sharp intake of air...inner thrust... outward release...mental stimulation a must as he whispers her name...his breath sensually

Glasses of a POET

tickles her back...giving that ass a nice firm smack...hands guiding and controlling hips...dick stretching and caressing lips...tip pounding pass walls on fire with liquid desire like scalding lava...seeking that special place...he can see the look on her face...the mirror was set just so...the shape of her mouth as she let's out an "ohhhhhh"...her tongue flicking, eyes swooning.. her lover spooning in her bowl like dipping for ice cream as the motion escalates, temperatures elevate, his rod hits and aggravates that g-spot...now she's really HOT...

He can feel his nut racing from the base...he slows the pace to accommodate but this chick all tight and thick is

Author R. Angel

throwing dat ass at an alarming rate...muscles vise-gripping his tool...Ooops he fucked up and got the fool...she really is taking him to school...he grabs a handful of hair...ready to take her there and goes for broke...measuring each forward stroke...giving her neck a tiny little choke...feeling the pre-orgasmic shudder that ran through them both...earth shaking the room in its' quaking...his explosion about to burst, but he's old block and she must cum first...fucking through the pain to refrain and her scorching rain...intent on his purpose and focused...he knew he was home when she cussed "dammit don't stop...this shit feels soooooo good"...he hit her nail hard with his driving wood...her body gave a jerk of

Glasses of a POET

climatic proportion...he knew
it was the moment to let go
the tension...his tongue traced
the sweat laced tracks and
they came together in blissful
climax...

Author R. Angel

The Mentor

Every time his words touch her, they leave his signature fingerprint on her soul etched in bold ink, sketched loud and clear...crystal and booming, he's been dressing and grooming her mind for something spectacular, keeps her thoughts draped in fine silks and mink...the elegance of black and the softest of pink...constant preparation...it is near...

He forces her to think outside the box of tradition...opening locks of the forbidden and scary....drink...and taste the extraordinary....nothing but the best is what he requires, igniting flames and starting fires that burn intensely and yearn for a mental intimacy that goes beyond the norm...

Glasses of a POET

calms each storm with the stern that captains this ship as pearls of wisdom drip from his lips...

Level after level, he reduces to ash devil after devil...commanding attention and respect, demanding the set and reset of the creative process, understanding a woman's need to be treated with equality and utmost dignity in the business game...nevertheless...knowing the two are far from the same...she must stand on her own feet and establish her own name...

His intellect and perpetual care is a Godsend sent to mend and repair the brokenness she once embraced...the heartache and tears traced before he came to lace her with newness and

Author R. Angel

ordained purpose. To elevate her to a place unforeseen by others, though hinted at by another...The awakening has begun, ushering in brightness only rivaled by the sun in all its glory... in his words, he has re-written her story...

Glasses of a POET

Shadows

I walk through the valley of the shadow of death fearing no evil...for my God has summoned the retrieval of the enemy's hordes and arrows meant for my doom and held all at bay...the gloom has vanished, chased away by His Spirit and the power of His might...demonic minions took flight, dreading the sight of His glory in the hour of my need. With great care and speed, He has heeded my call to drive them all back against the impenetrable wall of His love for me. I am His child you see, a child of the King and it is no strange thing that a Father as compassionate as He would come to His daughter's rescue and if He

Author R. Angel

has done it for me, He'll surely do it for you...

The enemy comes like a thief in the night...bringing trouble, confusion and attempting strife...spreading darkness and chaos to add to the stresses of life but I know a Light that will slice through the dark, leaving the mark and blood of the Son whose work was done on that old rugged cross...He paid the cost for my freedom and yours, for us to walk freely and bold through the doors and enter the very throne-room of our awesome King so in your time of trial, lift your voices and sing...We have an advocate, a High-Priest who feels our pain and despite the schemes of the enemy, forever He shall reign...high and exalted with a name above all names...

Glasses of a POET

So, I walk through this valley full of shadows of empty threats...challenging my mind and thoughts to live free of vain regrets and past memories of ill misdeeds...on lies, drama and foolishness it constantly, willfully feeds but I have found a Savior who fought and took back the keys and the Word says that "whom He has freed is truly free indeed..." So find you a quiet, comfortable spot, whether standing or on your knees, and spend some time with the Creator who controls all the powers that be...

Author R. Angel

Honey Do Expression

Honey can u do me, like you do when you do what you do to make my honey drip from my lips to your lips as the tip of your tongue mingles with the juice of my passion fruit and you wipe my list clean with a mean lick and a swipe...you never leave a mess as my thighs caress your chest and I handle my homework down south...yo girl has a dirty mouth but you wash it out with your spray hose no doubt...we get caught up in this 69, forget the time in the swirl and mist of checking off shit on our honey do list...

Glasses of a POET

Mental Expression

Rose colored sheets of blush and thrusts that magnify your pen strokes...the lust of ink's passion stokes the fire of words like hot intimate intercourse as pen and paper coerce and mingle...the creative juices flow and tingle around wet edges of ink spots and intellectual thighs rise to your enterprise...delving into deep places of thought and mind to combine the divine pleasures of discourse... all drenched and moist from the mental tangle...hitting curves from every angle with the power of your pounding quill...sending a resounding chill up spines and riding rhymes like waves...you intensify the motion of my ocean of consonants and nouns as my sheet screams

Author R. Angel

with a scented gush...the
round of my mound quivers
from your pens final rush..

Glasses of a POET

Ashes to Rebirth

Sleep walking through this reality nightmare that could so easily go either way...anticipating the light of daybreak and wanting to make the phantoms and ghost...the countless host of horrors that threaten to smear the quality of life disappear with the sunrise...juggling the lows and highs of disappointments, enjoyments and moments of possibilities gone wrong in this dance and song of every day living...taking and giving with entities real and imagined...hoping the sun's rays will burn a hole in this mold of depression that encloses me before it decomposes me and I have no existence or resistance left to make my great escape...

Author R. Angel

Plotting within this hollow shell...my thoughts take shape and drape my consciousness with the need to test the waters outside the zones of comfort that support my paralyzation...aching for some demonstration that faith is alive and well on the other side of this hell where I dwell daily...I can no longer just wait for death to come for me...I must chance this ride, embrace the hands of fate, swallow useless pride, scraping these ashes of empty words and broken promises away to start with a fresh plate...a clean slate...a new due date...

Rebirth...for I will be reborn...I will take what is ripped and torn and put the pieces together again...mend

Glasses of a POET

the broken and heal the sick...repair the breach in my mind, restore what was lost in time and sway to the rhythm of an original rhyme...demand the return of that which was stolen, cease the controlling of my actions by some alien force...send divorce papers to my fear...the bullshit stops here...in my strongest voice I decree...it's time to let it burn for me...

Author R. Angel

Dream Lover

Intimacy expressed in
fantasies and unholy glimpses
of thoughts bound for Sin...the
Lion's Den hungry for the
taste of sweet flesh, ripe
mounds of breasts and
luscious inner thighs...soft
moans and cries of imagined
passion and dreams
that seem so real as to project
the feel of touch and smell...

The fingers, they linger on
skin burning,
yearning...midnight turning
into day
but doesn't melt away the
longing within...the turbulent
spin of bodies colliding, hips
and hands gliding, lips dip and
return with drips of honey
nectar...precious juice
produced from the seduction
of sensual sleep...the roaming

Glasses of a POET

of tongues deep and
probing...the ultimate
disrobing as she twist restless
upon sheets...I'm describing
her nightmare as the rhythm
repeats...can't you tell...

Sweat beads as palm needs the
perk tip of her mountain
tops...drip drops, drip drops...
the bed is drenched...clench
and un-clench,working her
body like a tool and wrench...
a ringing from far away...she
flinches, closer...closer...closer
it nears...eyes moist with
tears blink...her flow has
spilled to cover paper thin
sheets like ink...another jerk
and
she awakes...her body still
shakes and quakes from the
fire her lover has creamed...
intimacy expressed itself in
fantasy...her soul has been

Author R. Angel

redeemed...her orgasm was true...
her lover was dreamed.

Glasses of a POET

Playful Expression

Civil war between your heart and mind...the time to grind has cum and I am enjoying the feel of each battle scar laid lusciously against my skin...your hardened sword at the ready...to plunge into the soft wet marshes between the hills that are my thighs...your eyes drinking in the sin of me as I open to you the treasures of plundered booty...hazy as you gaze at the spoils of your victory... the prize and trophy of a hard fought campaign...my body the glass holding the champagne of your triumphant entrance into this city sieged by the strong grip of your hand and the sure pounding of your battle ram...you laid waste every fortified wall...your battle cry..my siren call as your

Author R. Angel

soldier stands at attention, prepared to release his honorable discharge...my war mound shivers and quivers...awaiting your heroic and forceful barge into the gates of the reward you claim...I anticipate losing yet winning this particular war game.

Glasses of a POET

<u>Gold</u>

If dick was a gold mine, I'd mint you...sin again and again then repent after I

knocked your socks off and rocked then Fort Knoxed you

If dick was a gold mine, I'd be plenty rich with infinite gold coin to satisfy my itch

and the twitch I get to spend it fast...If dick was a gold mine, I'd mint that ass

and lock it tight in a vault...not my damn fault but good gold is hard to come by and

I'm sold on that good shine you leave behind when you wax my pa-tussy...so...

If dick was a gold mine..I'd mint you and stake my

claim...buy up some beribonds in

my maiden name and have
your head stamped on every
golden piece...my own private

stock set aside for my release...

If dick was a gold mine...it's
yours that I would mint...but
since it's not and you forgot...

your time has all been spent...

Glasses of a POET

CRUSHED

I watched the door slam on my happiness again

and I was

Crushed

game and chasing fame, you made a decision

that left me

Crushed

The division growing wider and I'm growing wiser with every

minute and feeling of being

Crushed

The tell-tale signs of you inside her and your constant cheating

relentless in your unconcern about my being

Author R. Angel

Crushed

The lies and empty promises that meant less to your unrepentant

heart while my pride stayed

Crushed

And that bullshit part you played like I did some wrong to you when I finally

opened my eyes and revised my fucking plans cause I got tired of being

Crushed

So now the shoe is hurting the other foot...is it too tight or have you realized

the foolishness of your plight when you was dipping and slipping all night,

leaving me at home

Crushed

Glasses of a POET

You grieving over the good you had that you turned bad and the thought of him

gripping my thighs as my hips rise to the touch of his embrace...you won the

prize but you lost the race in the pace of your own tripping, so the canvas awaits

the stroke of a different brush...he takes his time, he's never rushed...gentle

strokes that bring out my natural flush...all because you wanted to know how

it feels to be...

Crushed

Author R. Angel

Expression of Illusion

The illusion and confusion in sex is love...the delusion in the fusion of two bodies that meet and greet one another is that they actually care for each other...that they render and surrender in some deeper feeling and not acknowledge that each thrust is produced by lust and nothing more...panties and belts slung hastily to the floor is not a statement of bedroom love in fashion but of passion, wanting and blind...he wanted that ass, u wanted it from behind...
Now u tripping on some love shit and he thinking you have lost your mind...

The reality and clarity of love is this...sex is a gift and we are defenseless against its

Glasses of a POET

awesome power...its wanton push in the midnight hour...its allure and pure seductive bliss but please don't confuse love with the hit and miss...Let me hit you then miss you is a sexual game and a many innocent heart lies at its feet to claim...so if love is the jewel in your crown you seek...be mindful of the sweet mouth and sleek talk that will have you taking that on the plank walk and diving into the very pits of hell...that place they used to call "heartbreak hotel"...

If true love is your goal and desire...stay clear of passion's burn and the fire...stay true to your heart and only that which you yearn cause passion is sweet going down but it makes the insides churn... without true love..

Author R. Angel

Love's Embrace

He stripped her bare, removing the layers of dead emotion and hurt like dirt and dried skin with the love within him, like a powerful exfoliant...penetrating flesh, bone, heart and soul...the wind cold to her exposed being but she trusted him, seeing the care with which he peeled away the debris and decay...

Years of misuse and ill treatment shedding at her feet on a street corner in an unfamiliar space yet a known place because she was with him...surrounded by sound and human activity yet lost in a secret world built for two...this the reality she had longed for, yet unprepared for each tear that ripped and

Glasses of a POET

released her pain so her peace could soar...

He knew the price being paid...she had yet to see the plans laid and the road paved by his actions...she was raw and tingling...her tears mingling with the warmth of his breath and reaction to her feelings...the moon shone bright, her mind reeling with thoughts of life and death...something was being buried in all that old earth at her feet, making way for a rebirth...
Then, with infinite tenderness, he covered her in the warmth and full protection of his loving embrace, draped and laced her in value, retracing each step in the process of removal, adding renewal of life in each touch...knowing what she needed much more

Author R. Angel

than she, he took her past physical intimacy to a realm of pure spirituality, showing her with his deeds and eyes just how prized and loved she really was...

Fantasy ceased to exist with a gentle kiss on the cheek, arms hard and strong yet so soft and reassuring held her tight, enduring his sacrifice and decisions made, he walked away into the night, leaving her fully clothed and saved from the heaviness of crossing a forbidden line...his own thoughts heavy on his mind but knowing she was glowing from the inside out...without any frets or doubt about tomorrow...

He stripped her bare...then covered her in the warmth and full protection of his loving

Glasses of a POET

embrace...he walked away, leaving her fully clothed and free from all regrets and sorrow...

Author R. Angel

Dead End Expression

She said, "you reject loving me so u can love me... That is so sweet it hurts..."

He responded, "you want one or the other.. One is a dead end road...That we both know won't work..."

Glasses of a POET

About R. Angel

Kim Morrow (known as Author R. Angel) is the mother of two. Born in Baltimore, she lives with her family in Reidsville, North Carolina, which has been home most of her life.

Kim Morrow is a Paralegal by profession, but reading and creative writing have always been her first loves. She published her first work of poetry in 2001, and after several rejections from publishers, she had given up on writing as a career.

However, a life altering event changed that and Kim published her first novel Dark Family Secretz in 2012 and the revised version in Feb 2014. Since **Dark Family Secretz**, Kim has self- published four more titles: **STEAM ROOM BLACK, HEAT'S DESIRE PARTS I AND II**, and a short book of erotic poetry, **DIP IN MY INK**.

Author R. Angel

In March 2013, Kim successfully launched her own publishing company BlaqRayn Publishing and Promotions with the publication of **THE UNPOLISHED GEM** by Author Benjamin Davis and **FENCES** by Author/Motivational Speaker Jerri Duncan-Hansen. She has also published 3 more poetry titles: **NightScapes: The Midnight Hour of Poetry, Red Shoes and Sex: An Erotic Journey and Deep Dark Delicious. Glasses of a Poet** is her 5th poetry title.

Glasses of a POET

BOOKS BY R. ANGEL

FICTION:

DARK FAMILY SECRETZ

STEAM ROOM BLACK

HEAT'S DESIRE PARTS I AND II

POETRY:

Dip In My Ink

NightScapes: The Midnight Hour of Poetry

Red Shoes and Sex: An Erotic Journey

Deep Dark Delicious

Glasses of a Poet

Author R. Angel

Author R. Angel

www.ingramcontent.com/pod-product-compliance
Lightning Source LLC
Chambersburg PA
CBHW071518040426
42444CB00008B/1708